Disney MOVIE MAGIC

This book is designed to be used with the following instrumental publications:

00841178	Violin
00841179	Viola
00841180	Cello

ISBN 978-0-7935-7843-6

HAL•LEONARD®
CORPORATION
7777 W. BLUEMOUND RD. P.O. BOX 13819 MILWAUKEE, WI 53213

OUT OF THIN AIR
from Walt Disney's ALADDIN AND THE KING OF THIEVES

Words and Music by
DAVID FRIEDMAN

Can You Feel the Love Tonight

from Walt Disney Pictures' THE LION KING

Music by ELTON JOHN
Lyrics by TIM RICE

CIRCLE OF LIFE

from Walt Disney Pictures' THE LION KING

Music by ELTON JOHN
Lyrics by TIM RICE

Moderately (with an African beat)

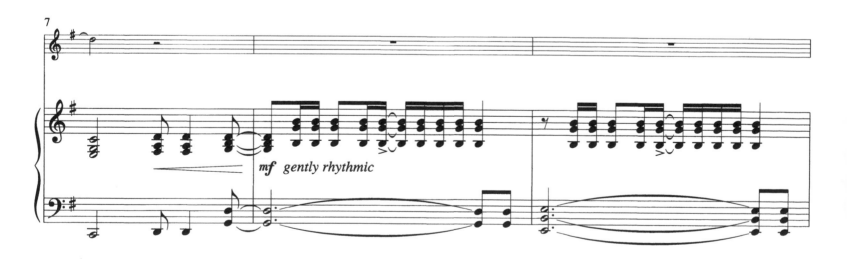

HAKUNA MATATA

from Walt Disney Pictures' THE LION KING

Music by ELTON JOHN
Lyrics by TIM RICE

I JUST CAN'T WAIT TO BE KING

from Walt Disney Pictures' THE LION KING

Music by ELTON JOHN
Lyrics by TIM RICE

THIS LAND

from Walt Disney Pictures' THE LION KING

Music by
HANS ZIMMER

CRUELLA DE VIL

from Walt Disney's 101 DALMATIANS

Words and Music by
MEL LEVEN

COLORS OF THE WIND

from Walt Disney's POCAHONTAS

Music by ALAN MENKEN
Lyrics by STEPHEN SCHWARTZ

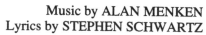

26

D.S. al Coda

⊕ CODA

JUST AROUND THE RIVERBEND

from Walt Disney's POCAHONTAS

Music by ALAN MENKEN
Lyrics by STEPHEN SCHWARTZ

D.S. al Coda

CODA

Meno mosso - freely

Piu mosso

THE VIRGINIA COMPANY

from Walt Disney's POCAHONTAS

Music by ALAN MENKEN
Lyrics by STEPHEN SCHWARTZ

MINE, MINE, MINE

from Walt Disney's POCAHONTAS

Music by ALAN MENKEN
Lyrics by STEPHEN SCHWARTZ

Madrigal style

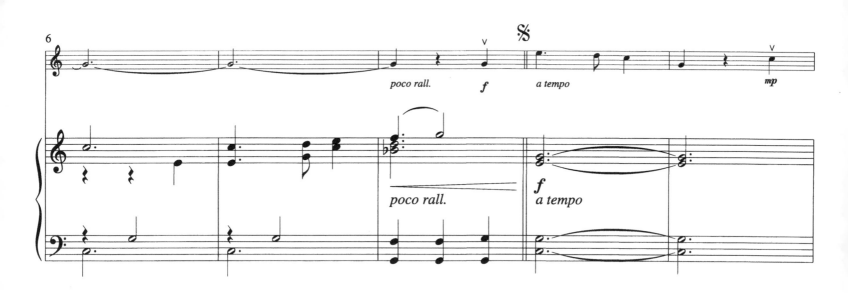

CODA

FORGET ABOUT LOVE

from Walt Disney's THE RETURN OF JAFAR

Words and Music by
MICHAEL SILVERSHER and PATTY SILVERSHER

STRANGE THINGS

from Walt Disney's TOY STORY

Music and Lyrics by
RANDY NEWMAN

YOU'VE GOT A FRIEND IN ME

from Walt Disney's TOY STORY

Music and Lyrics by
RANDY NEWMAN